MANISH!

MANISH!

new poetry by
Alfred L. Woods

Third World Press
Chicago

Man'ish (man ish), adj. Resembling, suitable to, or characteristic of a man; manlike, Syn. See MALE - man'nish ly, adv. - man nish ness, n.

Copyright 1989 by Alfred L. Woods
2nd. Printing 1991
Published by Third World Press
7524 S. Cottage Grove Ave. Chicago
All Rights Reserved
Printed and Bound in the
United States of America
ISBN:0-88378-122-0

Drawings by Robert Glover are on pages 15, 22, 36, and 49.
Drawings by Steve Walker are on pages 11, 13, 24, 27, 35, and 43.

Cover design by Steve Walker
Cover photograph by Franklin Huggins
Book design by Michael Hudson

Grateful acknowledgment is made to the following publications in
which some of these poems have appeared:FORMAT, NIT & WIT,
RHINO, SYNCLINE, INPRINT, READING FROM THE IWI CON-
FERENCE, HAYMARKET, HANGING LOOSE, & THE CHICAGO
OBSERVER, CONVERSATION is printed through the courtesy of
Johnson Publishing Company.

This publication is supported by a Community Arts Assistance Project Grant from the
Chicago Office of Fine Arts and the Illinois Arts Council/Expansion Arts Program.

dicated to my dreammakers, my dreamkeepers,
and my dreams come true.

How many winters have gone down
to the yard from my window

When you are young, everything is unlimited and always.
But lately, I've been chewing jellybeans slower.
Even the once-hated licorice I can enjoy when I chew
it for a year or two. And I've been searching hard
to find blues in snapshots that are as purple as
the asters I brought you but not the blue of indigo.

The colors of teakwood, ebony, Boston coffee, and
burnt umber are the colors that I associate with
our bodies lying side by side or entangled
in a feverish yet preposterous position never reproduced
as one of the one hundred positions depicted in
those illustrated sex manuals because they never
show us making love. It's our position. And I've
begun to look more at your cheeks, your brows, and
your back while searching frantically for a simile
or blues song to fix you in my mind. It will be our
song. The angles of your face and head, the valleys
of your back, belly, your thick thighs and buttocks
I outline lightly with a finger and closing my eyes
I trace you in the dark to further impress this into
my mind.

Baby, lately I've been doing things less often and
more slowly, wanting instead of a thousand and one
nights to remember to have learned this night as
slowly you already withdraw from me to slip away
into soft memories like those childhood winters that
fell down gently to the yard from my window.

Then I slept
with your heart cupped
resting softly
in my palm
in a sleep disturbed
only by the odor of
strong musky hair
breathing in a long
warm eternity . . .
the night.
Night sounds roused
you
and I had a need
to drink
but we moved
not to disturb
Andromeda.
Finally,
then I slept
with your heart
a black comet
bursting through
my finger tips.

9

Very, Very Varied

Jamella walked out the room . . .
the color of an eggplant or olive
was the bathroom light on her
shoulder and cheeks.

Francine, black hair marcelled and
finger waved, walked into the
bedroom, the color of an egg yolk
was the excitement in her eyes.

I rolled away from Ruby's breasts
that were the perfect shape of two
greased pecan shells and thought about
southern women who walk in faded
print dresses barefoot down dirt roads

not bothering to carry a purse so
sure are they of where they are going
and thought about Samella who walked
into my bedroom licking philodendron
lips and smelling like black walnuts.

I have seen the autumn climax of
maples, oaks, and sycamores on the
streets of Chicago and knew them as
Mable Lyn, Ora, and Saffron . . .
the leggy vary-colored girls who
walk in and out of my room.

to TM

last night
hearing a voice behind me say
hello I turned
hope filled
only to have it turned to stone
it was inside me

But this above all we had to admit —
    sitting in the cool dark damp
    basement like primeval man
    sitting on silent nights around
    a camp fire but allowing the
point of our manhood to rest on the
    foundation of whose was the biggest
    and in the act of doing so
    drew lots for who would be
    the first to take her — Jamaica
    was cool.
When now we open the door to memory
    and watch balls of our hair
    like tumbleweed rolling across
    parched deserts, roll before us
bouncing softly against memories that   11
then promised such tangible joy we damn her.

Time has not diminished the pleasure
    we took in just watching her,
    following her through streets
    and alleys. All summer she
wore pink and purple print blouses
    tied bolero style under cool
    soft swells and shorts, shorts
    that were a pair of hot moist
    hands caressing her
And as the hot august days lanquished
Jamaica remained cool and unconquered.

Damn Jamaica anyway, we say. She was
two damn cool. We still marvel
at the Coke top she wore in her
navel, fastened there in some
mysterious way. We often speculated
how it stayed there and what we
would do if we were it and we
damned it too. But the mystery
and the damnation only served to
increase our passion to drag her
into the basement screaming and
laughing and legs flaying the air trying
to kick the shit out of the biggest one
as down into the dark damp hole we carried her.
Now we speculate, as we watch balls
of hair tumble across the floor
moved by some mysterious force
that it was the rusty tops that she
wore in her navel that corrupted
with lockjaw our Jamaica. But
even in death Jamaica was cool. In
red roses, white lilacs, pink
lace, and death she smiled.
She smiled as we stood like primeval
man frail in black and silence
weeping down on her, letting
our tears quench our passion.

In Jamaica's memory we swore a silent
vendetta and like hunters we
retraced the jungle of streets
and alleys that Jamaica had walked
that summer and with vicious joy
we tracked down and drilled holes
through the center of every top we
found in payment for corrupting our
Jamaica and the tangible promise of
pleasure that she offered.

Desiree

I want you black
(black as a paper sack
I carry
so filled with nutrition
desire makes me hug it
with both arms feeling and
smelling its goodness,
I salivate).
I want you black
(black as a yellow peach
full as a harvest moon).
I want you black
(bluer than a blackberry
browner than black ivory
blacker than the red
I see when tight closed eyes
I conjure up your fading image).
I want you black.

Chicago

If this was New York I might be
taking the train from Syracuse,
Brooklyn, or Queens and not the
7:48 from South Shore to the Loop.

If this was New York I would have
to go on vacation to see the sun
rise over Lake Michigan swishing
silver-sequined past Hyde
Park, catch John Hope stopping to
admire the rose bushes lining the
Quadrangle Club, see Mies exercises
in glass and steel, or ride the
CTA looking over the shoulder of
the poet laureate who might explain
to me that she is on her way to
read her poems at The Tubman School
for Unwed Mothers but enroute she
talks to strangers and pulls dead
words from nowhere and orders them
with a felt tip pen on a legal pad
to be born again.

If this was New York there would be
high rises and sky scrapers fencing
it in, containing it, preventing it
from rolling unnoticeably in contrast
to anything except the harbor and the
lake, it would have no place to flow
into, I would be reluctant to enter
it aware that often in play it can
be dangerous, and it would be called
Central and not Grant Park.

Chicago Politics

If you looking for somebody
to be good to
Chicago is the place to start

If you looking for somebody
to be good to
Chicago is the place to start

But remember that while
the hot tongue of love
is getting comfortable
the barometer can take a dip
and a cold frigid breath
of wind can began to blast

So, when you stop over in Chicago
please fall in love real fast

I said when you stop over in Chicago
please fall in love real fast, and often

Because like the lake front wind gusts
Chicago love can change directions suddenly
and besides it ain't even guaranteed to last

The girl next door

She woke up wanting nothing endlessly
but a quiver upon the ether a
mere association growing in an
impossible and sometimes foolish place

She woke up feeling susceptible

She woke up wishing she was in a
strange situation inhaling
familiar but different odors
She woke up singing

She woke up singing your
love is a dandelion root
growing in impossible and
sometimes unwanted places   17

Growing into a stiff warm smile
a stiff smile
She woke up feeling susceptible

Happy Birthday Connie Blues

Tell me, how did you awake today little mama
pressing another year on your fine brown frame.
Tell me, how did you awake today little mama
pressing aonther year on your fine brown frame.

Patting memories into your biscuits or
pouring aspects of love into a pot of grits.

Happy birthday to you little mama
let each hour of your day make love to you.
Happy birthday to you little mama
let each hour of your day make love to you.

Let it fill you up with joy for tomorrow
to give you returns for your whole life through.

Happy birthday to you little mama
let each hour of your day make love to you;
let it fill you up with joy for tomorrow
to give you returns for your whole life through.

Slit up the side

Have you ever left
your bed
in the morning
wanting to
just reach out and
keep holding on
holding on to tomorrow
plus
all the fun you had
Have you ever left
your bed feeling
like you still had your
Saturday night shoes on
smiling at distractions
remembering
all the fun you had
moving to the beat
of unplayed music
remembering
all the fun you had
Have you ever gone to work
in the morning
two hours late
but still on time
smiling at distractions
remembering the fun you had
Have you ever gone through a
day still feeling
like a honeysuckle in need
of a bumble bee
in need of someone to
suck your sap
or at least a cool breeze
to shake your pollen free
Have you ever gone
through a day
feeling like desire
on a baby's face
and your only explanation
is I just woke up
feeling this way today

19

Let's do today
something ˙ talk about years later,
Annie Mae.
Let's play house
or search through
unrecorded dialog
of historical
follies lost.
. Let's do today
something
to rock with
laugh about
when we
sit patting our
feet sucking on
pieces of
memories recalled.
Let's do something
today,
Annie Mae.
Let's do something,
something
so long slowly.

20

Mulatto

The aura that surrounds a full moon is the
color of your skin, or, it is the clarity
of amber, sardonyx, opal, the white in the
heart of a honeysuckle rose, the red sour
clay from Mississippi, Alabama, and Georgia.

Your hair falls heavy to your shoulders like
strings of beads or it is tossed about your
face like heavy black thunderclouds but it
can be as pedestrian as lake-washed sand and
as unyielding as dried peanut vines.

And your walk is only the consequence of your
constant attempts to resist being used for
special effects.

We study it all the time or
seldom, noting the meandering Nile and
national boundaries; see it interpreted
on television and in the movies, read
about it in the newspapers. It is
dark; the continent of contrasts
and change; the continent
of violets, black
panthers, lush forests,
deserts and savage beasts.
In the National Geographic
it is a colorful land
of Bantu, Masai, Ubangi,
and Watusi; a land
of customs and
animals, nearly
extinct. But
on the Rand Mc-
Nally Atlas, Africa
is the size of the
heart, or a tear drop, or
of lead, or of oil,
copper, or rubber
or a drop of
platinum or coffee

23

THE LAW

You know what you did is the
only answer to our question as
our numbers march by legions into
the jails. Still virgin boys and
girls, fathers and mothers, and babies
so young wet nurses are hired to
keep them alive to serve out their
sentence of guilt are there.
It was a short infield pop-up
Waco was about to catch when the
two pink policemen ran huffing and
puffing onto the field, slamming him
to the ground and because his wrists were
too thin they handcuffed his elbows.
Somebody should have yelled, "Interference!"
From the back seat of the squad car
Waco, slobbering, cried to the peerage
of astonished spectators, "Go git daddy."
What is the crime my son has committed,
Mr. Watts asked the judge. Don't get
smart nigger, the judge yelled, you
know what he did!

Footnote
to the Assassination

April 4, 1968

but you've heard about him
time and time again. Time
and again, the Scottsboros,
the Tills, the Johnnie May's boys
and many many others
whose names were never known
but who were snatched to their
deaths by alleged and contrived
charges of criminal assault
on a white woman.

(hang it on him! hang it on him!
cried a 16 year old girl carrying
a baby, as Little Willie Floyd
approached the scaffold. Amid
a crowd of cheering white folks
little white boys and girls in
the crowd clap their hands in
eager anticipation of seeing
the trap door sprung and a once
youthful and radiant 22 year
old black man swing at the end
of a rope)

A crime was committed. A Negro
is arrested. Name never known.
The Scottsboros, The Tills, the
Johnnie May's boys,
and many many others whose
names were never known.
But you've heard about it.
A crime is committed.

Shop Talk

We see days filled
with the vacant glare of
three war veterans
wiggling the toe of a blown off foot
playing with their three ounces
of silence

The sons of soldiers trained in
Harlem backyards
to defeat the enemy and did
having never been taught
or tasted failure,
the sons of women redefining
the womb from which they push
challenge, directness, ambition,
self esteem, whose code names are
Wilson, Dominoe, Africannus Jones,
Willie Boy, and Sugar Babe

Are selecting the wars for which we
will battle and sending
regrets to others that do not
represent our cause.

Are dialing call-a-war
telling the operator not to
take any more messages
future generations are busy and
they will get back to them
two weeks from last Thursday
time away from wars is needed to
celebrate the fest for
children and fat cheeks

Are cultivating plants and
demanding caresses
are soft stroking on the
down beat
are singing songs to the
surging salty sound of
distant drums
are contemplating hairline cracks
and the distant rumble of
walls collapsing

We see days filled
with more than the vacant
glare of war veterans

Posthumous Song
of an Aborted Holiday

Once there was a summer of endless
record breaking natural disasters,
gang bangs, refrigerator and crib
deaths, and in Birmingham a church
was bombed every other Sunday as
a sacrificial offering to the moon
that had remained full for more
than four hundred years.

Once in the life of Jelly Roll,
winter brought not with it to
his and Baby Sister's cold water
flat pots steaming with catfish,
collards and hamhocks, rutabagas,
and corn bread, and in the streets
below it was not Jolly Saint Nick
and his eight tiny reindeer
Jelly Roll sometimes saw but a long
black hearse followed by a
lone black limousine.

Once, on a cold sunny day in November,
Jelly Roll, the paper boy, sat on
the window sill composing a suicide
note to Baby Sister, five months
pregnant and still in love, who sits
at the table following from the floor
up the cabinet and into the sink a
route of roaches who could be ants,
if this was summer.

"Once," he wrote, "this city had a lot
of heart but it ain't safe being out of
work and looking forward to Christmas and
birthdays makes me scared and it
feels like a pot boiled wool sweater
on my back when it used to be called
love and we wore it like Daddy's housecoat."

Jelly Roll sat on the window sill
composing a suicide note to Baby
Sister that he lullabyes her
to sleep with every Friday night.

The Jacob Syndrome

Like lately I've been having this recurring dream
about you and me trying to make it
and every time we try to do it
it's like this giant avalanche of snow
is blocking the door to the cabin
out in the wilderness that
we are trying hard to get out of

And the dream jumps back into a Cecil B. DeMille
super-scope and man I see it ain't even
a cabin in the wilderness as a matter
of fact there ain't even no wall
just this door with this
white avalanche blocking it and

It's like James Earl Jones barreled chest
with shoulders as broad as a 4 x 4
crossbeam and legs like toothpicks
in the arena with gladiators
and I can hear the crowds laughing
and they roar like the hawk
across Lake Michigan

But it ain't funny man because it
ain't James Earl Jones fighting gladiators,
pushing on that
door and that ain't no
avalanche
that's us man that's me and it ain't
no dream man
it's for real man, it's for real.

Moss Dunbar

Always in the library
awkward at court
remembers who he sat
with at lunchtime
next to in history
and remembers
one morning finding
a love note taped
on his locker door.
Moss Dunbar
at ease
with the gift
of potential
for the next schoolday
laid out his clothes
the night before
blue jeans and loafers
for Friday
hung for Monday
on the doorknob
the shirt and tie
he wore
to church on Sunday.
Moss Dunbar an
example of the race
with
eyes so bright
skin so clear
friends and neighbors
referred to others as
Moss' brown skin,
remembers the night
he went to bed
age seventeen
and woke up
an angry
young man.

School boys have obligations too

On the way to geography
he found a slender book of
poems
where a man lounged sleeping
taught him how to cross his legs
and invited him
to sip a glass of dry red wine
he will give it to you
maybe
with
a bookmark on the
love poem

Dressed to Kill

Still
he rises early to make ready
for work
His uniforms are rough
dried but clean
From his hips dangle
his handsome equipment
On weekends he wears the
fatigues of the soldier on furlough
swaggering through the strange
warm civic smiles of shoppers
and storeclerks
Is this game so much better
than regrets and strained smiles
at the employment office
What flights of fantasy does
the caged bird take
Some days he is the Good Humor Man
or business man or CTA conductor
or telephone repairman inspiring
the desire of children
he passes
playing street games
to be
like him when they
get grown

The Understanding

I see him every morning.
He nods . . . I smile . . .
I don't need a watch on
Monday through Friday I
see him I know I'm on time.
He smiles . . . I nod . . .
Carrying his school books
seriously high under his left arm
he strokes, as we pass, the fuzz
above his lip (not yet thick and stiff).
He smiles . . . I nod . . .
Some mornings I leave the house in
a whirl — throwing loose change
into my pockets, adjusting my tie,
putting on my glasses almost forgetting
my dentures, pulling on my gloves — but
once on the street I suddenly and casually
adjust my breathing to fit his gait.
He nods . . . I smile . . .
Other times, I have the time to brush
each remaining tooth properly, a hundred
strokes at least, clip my finger and
toe nails, brush my suit, shine my shoes but
always timing my departure to see his face.
Our eyes make contact.
He nods . . . I smile . . .
And day after day
year in and year out
as we have in the past
do now and will do forever . . .
He nods. I smile.

Early

I haven't conquered the power
of love
or said no to the will
to live,
I haven't visited every town listed in the
world atlas
or studied the routine life of ordinary
people in Taranto.*
I haven't counted all the
dollars in Liberia or
lonely eagles from
Tuskegee.
Here I am
with so much still to do
on my paper route
practicing my whistle
throwing my papers
walking towards the
rest of my life.

34

*During World War II Black air pilots
were stationed in Taranto, Italy and thus
it is another site of African-American history.

Ain't you terrible,
ain't you something,
getting up everyday
with a new dream
to come true.
Go on now and finish
building that pyramid
and then tell Daddy again
how a nation was conquered
because you cartwheeled
the Alps.
But don't use up all
your strength cutting up,
we still need you to show
us how to channel the
ocean's flow, so be careful
now and don't hurt yourself
showing off.

35

If you are on your way
to being somebody
you must be in Chicago.
Chicago is the place to be
on your way to being . . .
being in love or on the
success rung up
and always forever young
with one hundred thousand
first things in your life
still to do
in your life
still to be
Chicago is the place
to be.

Chicago is the city . . .
the city of never been done
things to do
like turning a dream into gold
turning strangers into neighbors
each brief hot summer when
that's just something else
to do but politics is
a Chicago love affair.

So if you are on your way
to being in love or
on the rung up or
always forever young
with so many first things
in your life still to do
in your life still to be,
if you are on your way
to being somebody
Chicago is the place
to be.

HEROES

Moderately dressed and
somewhat successful the
preacher leaves the pulpit,
the teacher leaves the classroom,
Jackie Robinson leaves
the stadium, Paul Robeson
leaves the stage,
Joe Louis leaves the arena.

For them a fanfare
for heroes
we play, a fanfare passed
from father to son
a fanfare sung by a
nursing mother as
she pushes yet another
child into the world.
"Don't you give up, son.
Don't you turn back," is
her going away gift.

Under his strong hands
the work started by
Charles White, W.C. Handy,
Paul Lawrence Dunbar,
and Jacob Lawrence continues,
amid peril and threatened
betrayal,
to conquer, to defeat
while magnifying
our dignity
magnificently.

38

More often than not
Chicago is
fresh turned
black top,
still wet,
if you will notice.

Especially in a pre-dawn
morning after a flash
summer rain
when somewhere you
can hear the first
one to leave his house
every morning slam
the door and start the
engine letting it idle
for a while to smoke a
cigarette until
he has organized his day
and the first bird song I
have always heard
since I was a newspaper
boy pushing my cart
through the streets and alleys of my
newspaper route in the
pre-urban renewal
mornings in Hyde Park,
you can still hear,
if you will notice.

39

Close your eyes
to hear the toot of
a train whistle passing
through this urban country
town and the soft southern
drawl as twang of folks on
the southside of Chicago
wish you a 'hi'
or gentle 'howdy do,'
when they will.

Wars and urban ghettoes,
street gangs
and Chicago politics
do not seem to be as near
or matter much
when standing on the corner
your lungs take a strong dose
of the smell of Chicago,
still wet,
like fresh turned
black top,
if you will
notice.

Something is a fine
place to be.
Somehow is a steaming
pot of soup where
always, whenever, and forever
stew.
From the center is a warm place
to go especially
when you get wherever
and need to share
sometimes with nobody
something beautiful
and rare.
Then, especially,
something is a fine place to be.

Alexander, Alexander
(for d.a.b.)

Suddenly you realize, every year it happens.
Always, it seems, sometime in August a chill
in the morning air; maybe a shift in the shadows
cast by the early morning sun rays against
the juniper trees and the dry rustle the
leaves make tell you that although the forecast
is for record highs, summer is over. Regret
and anxious anticipation are not what the day becomes
but just a day full of awareness to detail.

On campus, you notice, in squads, packs, and
herds young boys like milk-fed studs or satyrs
tease and nip the premature autumn air.
Slim-hipped, broad-chested, narrow-waisted, their
girlish giggles and alto shrills like joyous music

is infectious. Their thighs ripple in sport,
you notice, and could part the way to exert force.
Their arms flex in midair to hurl a football and
could a javelin or circle and squeeze in play and
game a slightly resisting waist. Between their
games of dare and bravado they strut, pose, profile,
and pull on their long black moustache. Their
stiff long black moustache of tomorrow they pull
seeming to sing, "Nothing is over but something
has just begun."

Listen! Their voices call and their bodies stir
in the breeze. Stop! Can you continue your
walk home from the library already cataloging the
many different ways you will spend sweating
out the winter?

I have known a southern town
or state of mind where the
rain falls still on rooftops
made of tin and when the wind
blows, the door jams whistle and
whine.

I have known a southern town
or state of mind where women
believe in love at first sight,
love potions, and acts of God,
where men kill in a fit of
jealous rage, and children,
born of love, squat in the
field to smell turned soil
and buttercups.

43

Walk With Me.

The Quiet.
The Silence.

It creates a need in me
not to take lightly blizzards,
cloud formations, the perfume
of bruised rose petals, the
swish of nylon stockings,
firm backs, thick necks, and
full moons.

It creates a need not to
forget to get a haircut
every two weeks, shine my shoes,
clean my nails, walk backwards
across the path of black cats,
give to the African Missionary Society
and the Urban League.

The silence in *Ponciana* and
Sketches of Spain like the
vacant lots in Woodlawn, South Shore
and Grand Boulevard, or news of the
first reported crack in Lady Day's voice
create a need in me . . . a need
rocks cannot hide, a need
water will not satisfy,
a need rain cannot wash away.

This has nothing to do
with April

As you depart for the
newest dance step
I hope your trip is as
full as mine,
filled with bebop,
cool jazz, Stevie,
Ray Charles, and Leotyne Price and
as long as a fine
Brownskin Holiday.

I hope your trip is a long one
filled with church fans, ports
of trade, and a sky free of clouds.
May you visit Kenya, Haiti,
Chicago, and Birmingham
from their rhythm learn
and go on learning.

As you depart for the newest
dance step please don't hurry the journey,
so you are old by the time
you reach the dance floor
wealthy with all you have gained
not expecting dance and the music
of our people to have made you rich.

Jazz, bebop, and the blues
gave you that marvelous journey
without it you would not have set out
and if you find it troubling and
sad sometimes music will not have
fooled you
wise as you will have become
so full of experience
you will understand by then
what this music and dance is all about.

Hello goodby, first

Did you become somebody else's
miracle, his dream come true,
like a suddenly seen
penny in the street days
of my youth?
Each autumn for sixty years
or more I walk those streets
looking for the penny
I should have pocketed,
searching through
ten thousand shades of brown
ten thousand colors of tan
for a bright copper colored
penny I passed
on the streets in my youth.
Your name
I'll never know or
call out in the night.
Your brown skin
holiday
I'll never kiss or
turning my back say,
goodnight.

46

The fig tree she planted
before your first birthday
was also her gift
to you I recalled,
bending to pick up the
clenched hand of a
brownskin baby doll.

The fruit of that tree
feeds the honeybees and
hummingbirds and who
knows who else.
To whose touch did
this brownskin baby
doll bring nourishment,
a fragment of which I
discovered cutting across
a corner vacant lot.

47

Hardly abandoned, I think.
How long your little girl
or boy must have cried
when you could not be
mended and what was given
to him or her as a consolation,
I will never know,
for a broken brownskin
baby doll.

The vacant lot only gives
this brown fist
that I
pocket like stolen fruit
to take home
where on my desk
like a talisman it
rests with the statue
of two struggling gladiators
and one ebony Watusi warrior.

a kind
of Thanksgiving

Autumn heroes
red hot coffee
paper sack tan
ablaze in the
parks idle
and linger along
the asphalt streets,
was it the summer sun
so hot it pained . . .
the frost now, that
set your leaves aflame?
Or, was it a
spring step
passing in a rush
on somebody's way
to being not here
that made your colors
my favorite time of the year?
Your stiff dark trunks
your strong limbs
autumn heroes;
sway from the
burden of bearing
bend from the burden
of carrying sleeping
spring dreams
and sweet brown skin
fruit
that is
harvested
thankfully.

Civilization
South of the River

The river flows in from the lake.
Its waves have washed up to all
the heroes of history.
DuSable was
the first.
Civilization south of
the Chicago River is
lined with store front churches,
carryout barbecue joints, and
Chinese restaurants.
Vacant lots and once stately mansions
gossip eternally about the
gay blades, Bronzeville days,
and the Jones boys. Civilization
is where the wind is the
swish of satin gowns and
lightly perfumed summer furs.
All day and half the night
the thump from schoolyard
basketball games seeds the rainclouds
and children laughing become a
retreat until the pain
from a white hot ember
is comfortable again
until a mouth full of sour
memories is sweet
until the age of malaise is
a june bug summer of yellow melon
memories induced by three
tumblers of bourbon.
I remember the Regal
and Sam Cooke . . . standing
in a Chicago blizzard to see Ray Charles
and the Jewel Box Review,
a younger Martin and his newly
befriended co-marshal,
Malcolm X, waving from the
grandstand of the Bud Billekin Parade.
Their stance is burned into my fiber
although
I march to the music of a postponed
parade.
Should you laugh at me or the
corps of engineers reverse the river's flow,
I will not want.
There remains still always
bourbon, rainwater, and heroes.

Anchored knee deep in festive children ballooned
entangled by the tinny trap trap of the high school
marching bands the bitter sweet waltz from the
drum and bugle corps the spirit of the
Bud Billiken parade convinces me . . .
to escape from January in Chicago.

How can I preserve the warmth from this
long brownskin holiday through January . . .
these strong earth tones? How much of sundresses,
tight tank tops, bare legs, and straw hats, like
so many layers of fat, to last until the spring
must I consume?

Escape, escape! my shadow cast on the crystals of
an ice caked window.
Escape, escape! the icy limbs of leafless trees,
blizzards, and blinding snow storms that muffle
street traffic as it falls into front yards
where nobody makes snowmen anymore.

Yes, next year, before the White Sox's tickets
go up for sale, the Lake Meadow's art fair is
announced, and the rose garden begins to bud, before
the urban magic and beguile begins, I will plot . . .
to escape from January in Chicago.

51

Manish!

In the corner of a small space
legs spread eagle
he sits
arms gathered across his chest

Soon
as a rush of brown
autumn leaves
over the garden bed
he will spread
over himself and you

He smells
he smells like a bottle
of lemon based cologne spilled
in the locker room

Every other moment and day
he wears different
uncoordinated attitudes
seductive, defiant, manish
young girls adore him
go away or be still you
want to make him

Dashing into a light rain he is
a school boy who shoulders and shifts
fairytales and daydreams
carrying homework problems to school

In tight blue jeans and t-shirt
he sprawls on the back seat
of the bus boldly making eye contact
with suited matrons and approaching
men shy as cottonwood seeds

Standing he quickly composes
the image of himself for his walk
and his talk dangling a warm
invitation to go day tripping
from the corner of his smile
you have much to teach him
be calm

On warm autumn evenings at
Hyde Park and the lake his
shoulders hugging the lake shore
legs stretching to Canal Street
he tries to figure out his next
twenty or more years
he is not too young to be worried

Just a short season of evenings
in small spaces is all he has to .
conjure and conquer
forked roads, rough landings
and things that go bump in the dark

To the touch
aroused
he will stroke
and strike and strike until
rutabaga memories complete
in the rootcellar

In a small space
a history of his grandfather's wisdom
and antics I give to him as
Uncle Brother in the front
seat of our '61 Ventura
between traffic lights at
Cottage Grove and Hyde Park
advised me in a strong
soft voice firm enough to
echo in his children's walk
In the small space
In the small space

IF SOMETIMES BLUE

It's a hard time situation
set up to make you blue.
Sometimes, it's a hard time situation
set up to make you blue.
That's why Mama said she
baked up sweet cakes and
told Dad to come home
with good news.

She said, remember your good thing can
go bad sometimes
but
nothing goes bad always.
Remember, your good thing
can do bad sometimes, she said,
but
nothing goes bad always.
If a hard time situation gets
heavy chew on Mama's baked
memories recalling Dad's good news.

I said, people, sometimes
it's a hard time situation
set up to make you blue.
Sometimes it's a hard time situation
set up to make you blue.
That's why Mama said she
baked us sweet cakes and
told Dad to come home
each and every day with
some good news . . .
even if he had to fake it.

Since the center is filled with all the
apparent necessities, I fill the corners
and walls with all the accouterments of life . . .
greenery, statuary, and prints, subdued and
tastefully framed.

In the morning I put on a tie and fill
my day trying to make intelligent and
objective decisions, in the evening
I entertain a string of friends, drawing
on cigarettes held poised between witty
jokes, or I clean the closet, throwing
away still serviceable tab-collar shirts,
stovepipe pants, and saddle oxfords.

I have outgrown one fiancee, four lovers,   55
a robbery and television. I have held up
well. I marvel at my spontaneous responses to
broad smiles, toddling babies, smart alacky
teenagers, the dread of tomorrow's un-
certainties, and wonder at my no-fault
parents who with only a clue just chided
me when I complained about life's unfairness
with the constant refrain, "Just wait 'til
you get grown."

I am someplace I have never been
growing into an image of myself.

Also Available From Third World Press